At the Market

Contents

Nadine Golden

The Farmers' Market

Every day, everywhere, people **buy** and **sell** things.

Farmers bring fresh fruits and vegetables to sell at the farmers' **market**.

Other people sell homemade breads, jams, and pies. Shoppers enjoy buying food from the **producers**, the people who grew and made it.

The Supermarket

People shop at the supermarket, too. Here **consumers** can find fruits and vegetables that were grown nearby—and some that were grown far away.

Some food is frozen. Some is in cans.

Why do you think foods are sold this way?

What other **goods** can you buy in the supermarket?

Trucks deliver goods to the supermarket every day.

The Flower Market

This special market sells only one thing—flowers! People buy flowers to sell at their own flower shops.

What store owner do you think comes to shop at this special market?

The Flea Market

At the flea market, **vendors** sell both new and used goods. Shoppers come to look for old, interesting things and for **bargains**.

The **prices** are not always fixed. A buyer and seller might agree to reduce, or lower, the price of something.

The Crafts Fair

Many different goods are for sale at a crafts fair—toys, pottery, quilts, candles, and much more. Craftspeople make their things by hand, and then sell them at the fair.

Some things were made by people in faraway countries.

A soap maker cuts cakes of handmade soap.

The Mall

At the shopping mall, people can visit many stores—all under one roof. They can also find places to eat and relax.

Hundreds of workers are busy selling to **customers** in the large and small shops here.

Most malls are so big that you need a map to find your way around! Where do you think these shoppers want to go?

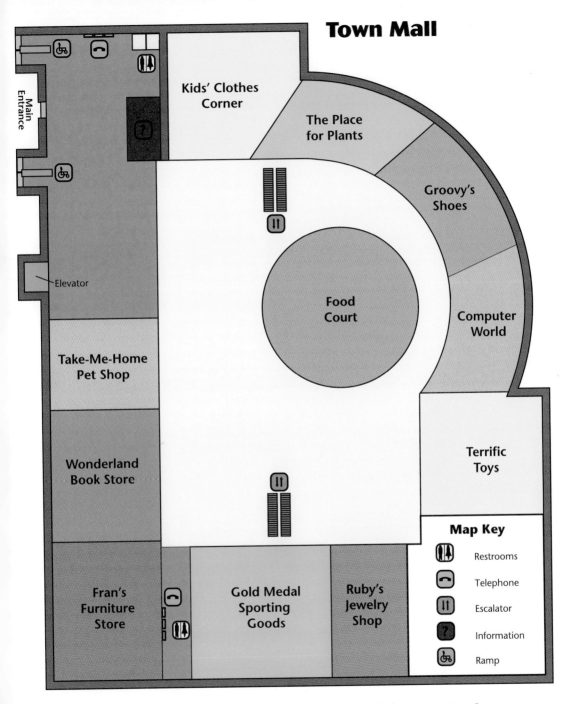

Town Mall

Main Entrance

Kids' Clothes Corner

The Place for Plants

Groovy's Shoes

Computer World

Elevator

Food Court

Take-Me-Home Pet Shop

Wonderland Book Store

Terrific Toys

Fran's Furniture Store

Gold Medal Sporting Goods

Ruby's Jewelry Shop

Map Key

🚻	Restrooms
☎	Telephone
↕	Escalator
?	Information
♿	Ramp

Find the entrance to this mall. Where would you go to have lunch? Where would you buy a gift?

Come to the Market!

How are these markets alike?

How are they different?

What other markets do you know?